The Sights and Sounds of New York's Chinatown

by Christine Wolf

Scott Foresman
is an imprint of

Glenview, Illinois • Boston, Massachusetts • Mesa, Arizona
Shoreview, Minnesota • Upper Saddle River, New Jersey

Every effort has been made to secure permission and provide appropriate credit for photographic material. The publisher deeply regrets any omission and pledges to correct errors called to its attention in subsequent editions.

Unless otherwise acknowledged, all photographs are the property of Pearson.

Photo locations denoted as follows: Top (T), Center (C), Bottom (B), Left (L), Right (R), Background (Bkgd)

Cover ©Stone/Getty Images; 1 ©Seth Wenig/Stringer/Reuters/Corbis; 3 ©Gail Mooney/ Corbis; 4 ©Stone/Getty Images; 5 ©MAPS.com/Corbis; 6 ©Phil Schermeister/Corbis; 7 ©ROB & SAS/Corbis; 9 (TR) ©Tim Pannell/Corbis; 9 (BL) ©Wolfgang Kaehler/Corbis; 10 ©Jerry Arcieri/Corbis; 12 ©Ramin Talaie/Corbis; 13 ©Seth Wenig/Stringer/Reuters/ Corbis; 14 ©Phil Schermeister/Corbis; 15 ©Richard T. Nowitz/Corbis;

ISBN 13: 978-0-328-39462-3
ISBN 10:   0-328-39462-9

1 2 3 4 5 6 7 8 9 10 V0G1 17 16 15 14 13 12 11 10 09 08

Have you ever been to China? You won't have to travel to Asia to see what it's like there. If you visit New York City's Chinatown, you will see the sights and hear the sounds of China.

In a tiny area in lower Manhattan, you will find many Chinese Americans. Their ancestors came to the United States from China. Their neighborhood in New York City is known as Chinatown. The sights and sounds of Chinatown make many people forget they are in an American city.

Chinatown takes up more than two square miles in New York City. Chinatown's streets are short, crooked, and **narrow**. They are usually crowded with people who live there and people who are just visiting.

Some of the people who live in Chinatown came to the United States from China. But others were born here in the United States. Either way, people in Chinatown keep Chinese history and culture alive.

What Sounds Will You Hear in Chinatown?

The sounds of people speaking Chinese can be heard throughout Chinatown. Some people in Chinatown do not speak English. English is a **foreign** language to them. Often, younger family members who know both English and Chinese help their older relatives.

What Traditions Will You See in Chinatown?

Many Chinese traditions are important to the people in Chinatown. Here are some.

TRADITION	REASON FOR
Bowing in front of elders	To show respect
Working hard	To honor and support the family
Practicing Tai Chi	To exercise the mind and body

Some older residents of Chinatown are disappointed in the younger generation. They see important Chinese traditions fading away. For example, today, many young Chinatown residents do not **bow** to show respect to their elders.

Older citizens of Chinatown sometimes think the young people are **foolish**. They wish the young would continue to practice Chinese traditions.

How Are Chinese Traditions Kept Alive?

Cooking traditional Chinese dishes is one way to keep the history and culture of China alive. In New York City's Chinatown, the street markets are filled with many choices. It is the same as in China.

The Moon Festival is a Chinese holiday of thankfulness. It is similar to our Thanksgiving holiday. A treat that is always served at the Moon Festival is moon cakes. They are made from a simple **recipe** of flour, milk, sugar, and eggs. Then they are decorated in many fancy ways.

Another Chinese tradition is celebrating the Chinese New Year. This holiday comes in January or February, depending on the year. No matter which month it comes in, the weather is sure to be **chilly**!

Chinatown's New Year's celebration brings plenty of excitement and crowds! There are parades, floats, street entertainers, and fireworks. Children receive gifts of money in small red envelopes. Sounds of drums, bells, and loud crowds fill the air.

To avoid the crowds, some people watch the celebrations from **perches** high above the city streets. They have a "bird's eye" view of all the action.

Chinatown is full of the colorful sounds, sights, and smells that make it like no other neighborhood in New York City and like no other place in the world!

Glossary

bow *v.* to bend the head or body to show respect.

chilly *adj.* slightly cold.

foolish *adj.* silly; not wise.

foreign *adj.* from a country other than your own.

narrow *adj.* having a small width; not very wide.

perches *n.* places to view things from high above.

recipe *n.* instructions for preparing something to eat.